THE BILLIONAIRE BIG BOYS

Strategies and Insights into the World of High-Net-Worth Individual's

RICHARD BENSON

TABLE OF CONTENTS

PRESENTATION

PRESENTATION

Who are the Billionaire Big Boys?
Recognized by their cosmic total assets and impact, these people length different enterprises — tech, finance, and then some. Each has a special excursion, however all offer the shared trait of exploring the intricacies of outrageous riches.

Welcome to the present show on "The Very rich person Huge Young men." In this investigation of uber abundance, we dive into the narratives, systems, and effect of people who have rose to the apex of monetary achievement.

Meet the titans who have formed businesses and reclassified achievement. From Jeff Bezos' online business realm to Warren Buffett's venture ability, we inspect the different ways that lead to the highest point of monetary accomplishment.

Investigate the extravagant way of life that goes with outrageous riches. From personal luxury planes taking off over the mists to palatial chateaus with all encompassing perspectives, the Tycoon Huge Young men exemplify a day to day existence where extravagance has no limits.

In a period overwhelmed by innovation, we spotlight the tech moguls who have amassed huge abundance as well as reshaped the computerized scene. From Elon Musk's endeavors into space to Check Zuckerberg's virtual entertainment domain, development is a sign of their prosperity.

As we finish up our excursion into the existences of these titans, recollect that the way to progress is just about as different as the people who track it. Whether you're thinking ambitiously or going for the gold, let the accounts of the Very rich person Enormous Young men move you to arrive at new levels.

Chapter 1

Investment Strategies of Billionaire Big Boys:

Lessons from the Wealth Titans""

Extremely rich person huge young men are proficient at differentiating their portfolios to moderate dangers. Investigate the different resource classes they put resources into, from customary stocks and bonds to elective speculations like land, confidential value, and funding.

One normal quality among extremely rich person financial backers is their drawn out viewpoint. Find how they weather conditions momentary market vacillations by zeroing in on supported development and keeping a patient viewpoint, and figure out how this way of thinking adds to their prosperity.

Extremely rich person huge young men are not risk-opposed; they are risk-cognizant. Uncover the gamble the board procedures they utilize, including careful expected level of effort, supporting methods, and reasonable plans of action taking that recognizes them in the venture scene.

Investigate how extremely rich person financial backers profit by market valuable open doors. Whether it's recognizing underestimated resources, upset showcases, or arising patterns, figure out how these insightful financial backers spot and hold onto rewarding venture possibilities.

Extremely rich person large young men influence state of the art innovation and information examination to illuminate their venture choices. Find how headways in man-made reasoning, AI, and large information assume a critical part in molding their venture systems.

Past monetary returns, a huge number designate critical assets to charity. Investigate how key humanitarian speculations add to cultural prosperity as well as line up with their more extensive venture methodologies.

Effective financial backers are light-footed because of changing economic situations. Analyze how tycoon huge young men adjust their venture systems to flourish in powerful conditions, exploring monetary moves and arising patterns.

Very rich person financial backers frequently have a worldwide viewpoint. Explore how they distinguish amazing open doors in various locales and markets, expanding their property to benefit from the interconnected idea of the worldwide economy

Maintainability is a developing thought for financial backers. Investigate how tycoon enormous young men incorporate ecological, social, and administration (ESG) factors into their speculation choices, mirroring a promise to long haul maintainability and dependable financial planning.

Extremely rich person financial backers perceive the significance of remaining informed. Find how they participate in constant getting the hang of, adjusting their speculation methodologies in light of developing business sector patterns, mechanical progressions, and international movements.

Chapter 2

The entrepreneurial mindset

How Billionaire Big Boys Build and Scale Businesses""

addresses a particular perspective and moving toward difficulties, epitomizing the remarkable arrangement of mentalities, ways of behaving, and abilities that drive people to recognize and benefit from open doors. In the present quickly developing business scene, described by mechanical progressions, globalization, and phenomenal vulnerability, developing a pioneering outlook is progressively perceived as a critical calculate making supported progress. This expert investigation dives into the center components of the pioneering outlook, revealing insight into its significance and the procedures people can utilize to cultivate and use this mentality for innovative achievement.

1 :Opportunity Acknowledgment: Business visionaries have a sharp capacity to distinguish potential open doors where others might see snags. They view difficulties as possible roads for advancement and development, continually looking for novel ways of making esteem on the lookout.

2: Hazard Resilience: An essential part of the pioneering mentality is a readiness to embrace risk. Business visionaries comprehend that carefully thought out plans of action are intrinsic to undertakings and are ready to explore vulnerabilities with strength and flexibility.

3: Proactiveness: The proactive idea of business visionaries separates them. As opposed to hanging tight for amazing chances to introduce themselves, people with a pioneering attitude effectively search out conceivable outcomes, step up, and make conditions helpful for progress.

4: Flexibility: The capacity to adjust to changing conditions is significant for innovative achievement. Business people are adaptable and open to changing their techniques in view of developing business sector elements, arising patterns, and unanticipated difficulties.

5: Imaginative Reasoning: Business people flourish with advancement, reliably rocking the boat and looking for creative answers for issues. They are ground breaking, utilizing imagination to foster items, administrations, or cycles that hang out in the serious scene.

6: Steadiness: The enterprising excursion is full of hindrances, and industriousness is a principal quality of those with an innovative outlook. Business visionaries view disappointments as learning open doors, staying determined chasing after their objectives.

Business visionaries focus on continuous learning and improvement. This includes remaining informed about industry patterns, mechanical headways, and developing customer inclinations to pursue informed choices and quickly jump all over arising chances, Building a strong expert organization is crucial for business visionaries.

Drawing in with similar people, guides, and industry specialists gives significant experiences, backing, and potential cooperation open doors.

Rather than dreading disappointment, business people embrace it as an intrinsic piece of the innovative excursion. Examining disappointments, gaining from botches, and applying these examples to future undertakings add to long haul achievement.

Fostering a pioneering mentality frequently requires a change in context. This incorporates reexamining difficulties as any open doors, seeing misfortunes as venturing stones, and keeping a positive and arrangement situated standpoint.

Business visionaries set clear, quantifiable, and reachable objectives. Separating long haul targets into more modest, significant advances considers better concentration, inspiration, and a feeling of achievement along the enterprising excursion.

The enterprising mentality is a strong impetus for progress in the present dynamic and cutthroat business climate. Developing this mentality includes a blend of inborn qualities and deliberate techniques pointed toward encouraging ceaseless learning, flexibility, and a proactive way to deal with valuable open doors and difficulties. As people embrace and assimilate the standards of the enterprising attitude, they position themselves to explore the intricacies of business as well as to flourish and improve in a consistently evolving commercial center.

Chapter 3

Luxury Real Estate Secrets

A Peek into the Property Portfolios of Billionaire Big Boys""

In the domain of land, the expression "extravagance" rises above simple lavishness; it epitomizes a way of life characterized by selectiveness, unrivaled solace, and modern style. Knowing purchasers and financial backers explore an extraordinary scene, where the securing of extravagance land includes a careful comprehension of industry mysteries. This article dives into the complexities of the extravagance housing market, revealing the mysteries that shape this restrictive area.

Understanding the Extravagance Housing Business sector: The extravagance housing market is described by its peculiarity, taking special care of a rich customer base looking for homes that rise above traditional norms. Dissimilar to customary land exchanges, extravagance properties frequently require a tactful methodology, with specialists and representatives utilizing an elevated degree of classification to safeguard the protection of the two purchasers and merchants. The way to exploring this selective market lies in understanding the nuanced factors that recognize extravagance exchanges.

Area, Extraordinariness, and Selectiveness: One of the premier insider facts of extravagance land is the accentuation on the spot. Prime districts with amazing perspectives, nearness to top of the line conveniences, and elite areas are principal. Extraordinariness adds to the charm; shortage upgrades esteem. Whether it's an isolated island retreat or a penthouse with all encompassing city sees, the shortage of such properties contributes fundamentally to their attractiveness.

Engineering Loftiness and Plan Greatness: Extravagance land rises above the common, with compositional magnificence and plan greatness at the front. Wonderful craftsmanship, cutting edge innovation, and tailor made completes are non-debatable components in extravagance homes. Planned purchasers frequently look for properties that mirror a combination of development and immortal style, organized flawlessly by famous draftsmen and originators.

Protection and Security: Security is a precious item in the extravagance housing market. Properties furnished with cutting edge security frameworks, gated doorways, and prudent formats are profoundly pursued. Secrecy in exchanges is similarly significant, with high-profile purchasers esteeming a cautious and secure cycle. Realtors proficient at protecting client security are priceless resources in this clandestine world.

Speculation Potential: Extravagance land isn't simply a home; it is a venture. Purchasers in this market fragment frequently look past the quick utility of the property, taking into account its true capacity for appreciation and long haul esteem. Understanding the financial elements, market patterns, and the extraordinary variables that impact the worth of extravagance land is a clear-cut advantage for the two purchasers and merchants.

Building Connections and Systems administration: In the domain of extravagance land, connections matter. Laying out trust, developing associations, and systems administration inside the princely local area are little-known techniques. High-total assets people frequently depend on suggestions and special interactions while entering the extravagance housing market, making relational abilities and a solid expert organization fundamental for realtors.

Extravagance land is a world regardless of anyone else's opinion, where classification, insight, and restrictiveness rule. Uncovering the privileged insights that support this market gives a guide to progress, whether you are a purchaser, dealer, or realtor. By understanding the nuanced components of area, compositional greatness, security, speculation potential, and the significance of connections, one can explore the extravagance land scene with artfulness and aptitude.

Chapter 4

Innovation and Disruption

Examining How Billionaire Big Boys Stay Ahead in Tech'

Development and disturbance have become vital parts of the contemporary business scene, molding ventures and reclassifying serious elements. In a quickly developing worldwide economy, associations that embrace advancement gain an upper hand as well as position themselves as drivers of progress. This talk digs into the significant exchange among advancement and disturbance, investigating their definitions, importance, and the essential objectives for organizations looking for supported achievement.

Characterizing Development and Disturbance: Advancement is the most common way of presenting groundbreaking thoughts, items, administrations, or cycles that achieve positive change or worth creation. It incorporates an expansive range, going from steady enhancements to notable headways. Then again, interruption alludes to the extraordinary impact that imaginative arrangements can have on existing business sectors, delivering conventional plans of action old and making completely new standards.

The Meaning of Development: Development is an impetus for development, empowering associations to adjust to changing business sector requests, remain in front of contenders, and meet the advancing necessities of clients. It cultivates a culture of nonstop improvement, empowering trial and error and gaining from disappointments. Also, advancement can drive functional proficiency, improve efficiency, and add to supportable works on, adjusting organizations to cultural and ecological assumptions.

Interruption as an Essential Power: Disturbance isn't simply a result of development; it very well may be a conscious technique for acquiring an upper hand. Organizations that effectively look to upset their ventures are many times described by a readiness to move ordinary standards and a guarantee to pushing the limits of what is conceivable. Troublesome developments can prompt the making of totally new business sectors, as seen with the approach of cell phones, which altered correspondence and media outlets.

The Job of Innovation: In the 21st hundred years, innovation fills in as an essential driver of both development and disturbance. Arising innovations like man-made brainpower, blockchain, and the Web of Things are reshaping ventures in all cases. Organizations that bridle these advances decisively can smooth out tasks, make new plans of action, and separate themselves on the lookout.

Advancement and disturbance are not secluded occasions but rather continuous cycles that shape the direction of organizations and businesses. Embracing a proactive position toward development and disturbance isn't only an essential decision; it is a basic for associations seeking to flourish in the dynamic and cutthroat scene of the 21st 100 years. The people who explore this landscape with prescience, dexterity, and a guarantee to pushing limits are ready to get by as well as to lead and reclassify the fate of business.

Vital Goals for Associations:

1: Develop a Culture of Advancement: Associations should cultivate a climate that energizes imagination, risk-taking, and nonstop improvement. This includes engaging workers to contribute thoughts, giving assets to innovative work, and embracing a mentality that values trial and error.

2: Put resources into Arising Advancements: Keeping up to date with mechanical progressions is fundamental for associations trying to improve and disturb. Key interests in innovative work, associations, and acquisitions can situate organizations at the front of arising patterns.

3: Dexterity and Versatility: notwithstanding interruption, authoritative nimbleness is urgent. Organizations should be ready to adjust rapidly to evolving conditions, whether it be shifts in buyer conduct, administrative changes, or the rise of new contenders.

4: Client Driven Approach: Understanding and answering client needs is basic to effective development. Organizations ought to effectively look for input, influence information examination, and utilize configuration figuring standards to make arrangements that reverberate with their ideal interest group.

Chapter 5

The Philanthropic Footprint

Exploring Billionaire Big Boys' Impact on Social Causes""

In the unique scene of magnanimity, the idea of a "magnanimous impression" has arisen as a critical structure for people, associations, and organizations trying to make an enduring and significant effect on society. The generous impression incorporates the complex components of magnanimous giving, underscoring the monetary commitments made as well as the essential methodology, manageability, and quantifiable results of altruistic undertakings.

Characterizing the Generous Impression:

At its center, the generous impression addresses the complete impact and impact that a donor or association leaves on the networks and causes they support. It goes past the customary measurements of dollars gave, taking into account the essential arrangement of magnanimous drives with all-encompassing cultural requirements and difficulties. This all encompassing methodology perceives that genuine effect requires a blend of monetary assets, smart preparation, and a pledge to driving positive change.

Vital Magnanimity:

One critical part of the magnanimous impression is the accentuation on essential altruism. Contributors are progressively perceiving the significance of adjusting their providing for clear cut objectives and results. This includes recognizing main points of contention, directing careful exploration, and teaming up with specialists and partners to foster designated mediations. By embracing an essential methodology, donors can boost the viability of their commitments and address main drivers instead of only easing side effects.

Estimating Effect:

A fundamental part of understanding and improving one's humanitarian impression is the thorough estimation of effect. Benefactors are presently putting a superior on proof based practices and information driven independent direction. By laying out clear measurements and assessment systems, givers can survey the substantial results of their drives, considering nonstop improvement and refinement of their techniques.

Maintainability and Long haul Responsibility:

A strong humanitarian impression reaches out past quick effects and embraces the idea of manageability. Humanitarians are progressively perceiving the requirement for long haul obligation to resolve fundamental issues. This includes monetary help as well as the development of organizations, limit working inside networks, and the cultivating of practical arrangements that can persevere past the underlying infusion of assets.

Innovation and Development:

In the contemporary charitable scene, innovation assumes a significant part in enhancing the generous impression. Advanced stages, blockchain, and information examination empower more proficient and straightforward giving, working with more prominent availability among benefactors and beneficiaries. Furthermore, developments, for example, influence money management and social business offer new roads for making positive change by joining monetary gets back with social and natural advantages.

The humanitarian impression addresses a change in perspective by they way we approach beneficent giving. As people and associations progressively perceive the interconnectedness of social, financial, and ecological difficulties, the requirement for a key, estimated, and reasonable way to deal with magnanimity becomes central. By scrupulously forming and growing their humanitarian impression, givers can contribute genuinely to the improvement of society, leaving an enduring tradition of positive change.

Chapter 6

Wealth Preservation Tactics

Insights from the Financial Playbooks of Billionaire Big Boys""

Abundance safeguarding is a critical part of monetary arranging that intends to secure and support resources for current and people in the future. As people amass abundance over the long haul, it becomes basic to execute key strategies to defend these resources from different dangers, like financial slumps, expansion, tax collection, and startling life altering situations. This article investigates key abundance protection strategies that people and families can utilize to guarantee the life span and security of their monetary inheritance.

Enhancement of Ventures:

One crucial procedure for abundance conservation is the broadening of speculations. Spreading resources across various resource classes, like stocks, securities, land, and elective ventures, mitigates the effect of a decline in a specific market. Expansion expects to adjust chance and prize, taking into consideration more steady and reliable returns over the long haul.

Domain Arranging:

Domain arranging assumes a critical part in abundance safeguarding by working with the consistent exchange of resources for main beneficiaries while limiting expense suggestions. Laying out an extensive home arrangement includes making wills, trusts, and other legitimate designs that obviously frame how resources ought to be disseminated. This not just guarantees that resources are passed on as indicated by the singular's desires yet additionally limits the weight of home expenses on beneficiaries.

Risk The board and Protection:

Judicious gamble the board includes distinguishing and moderating expected dangers to abundance. Satisfactory protection inclusion, including extra security, handicap protection, and obligation protection, can act as a defensive safeguard against unanticipated occasions. Via cautiously surveying protection needs and keeping up with fitting inclusion, people can safeguard their abundance from the monetary effect of crises or startling difficulties.

Charge Arranging:

Key assessment arranging is a basic piece of abundance conservation. People can upgrade their duty position by exploiting charge effective speculation vehicles, executing giving procedures, and remaining informed about changes in charge regulation. By limiting duty liabilities, people can save a bigger part of their abundance for them as well as their beneficiaries.

Long haul Monetary Preparation:

Abundance safeguarding requires a far reaching, long haul monetary arrangement that thinks about both present moment and long haul objectives. A very much built monetary arrangement considers factors, for example, retirement arranging, instruction subsidizing, and medical services costs. Ordinary audits and acclimations to the monetary arrangement guarantee that it stays lined up with developing monetary goals and economic situations.

Proficient Direction:

Connecting with the administrations of monetary consultants, bequest arranging lawyers, and expense experts can give important bits of knowledge and aptitude in abundance safeguarding. Experts can offer custom-made exhortation, explore complex monetary scenes, and assist people with settling on informed choices to really safeguard and develop their riches.

Abundance safeguarding is a dynamic and continuous interaction that requests cautious thought and proactive methodologies. By integrating a blend of expansion, home preparation, risk the board, charge arranging, long haul monetary preparation, and expert direction, people can improve the versatility of their monetary portfolios and make an enduring inheritance for people in the future. It is fundamental for approach abundance conservation with a comprehensive outlook, considering individual objectives, risk resistance, and the consistently changing monetary scene.

Chapter 7

Global Ventures

How Billionaire Big Boys Diversify Their Investment Portfolios""

In the unique scene of worldwide money, very rich people and institutional financial backers are continually looking for roads to streamline and differentiate their venture portfolios. The expression "Worldwide Endeavors" exemplifies the essential methodology attempted by high-total assets people to explore global business sectors and gain by arising potential open doors. This unpredictable cycle includes a careful choice of different resources, ventures, and geographic locales to relieve dangers and improve returns. In this complete investigation, we dig into the methodologies utilized by tycoon financial backers to broaden their portfolios on a worldwide scale.

The Basic of Broadening:

Expansion is a major rule in venture the board, stressing the significance of spreading speculations across various resource classes. Extremely rich people, with their huge monetary assets, frequently go past customary enhancement and embrace a worldwide point of view. This involves designating capital across a range of businesses, geographic locales, and resource types, decreasing openness to explicit dangers and market variances.

Global Speculations:

Very rich person financial backers perceive the worth of global openness in their portfolios. This involves putting resources into worldwide stocks as well as thinking about open doors in developing business sectors and different areas. Land, innovation, energy, and medical care are among the areas that draw in significant worldwide ventures. This essential methodology assists very rich people with profiting by monetary development in various districts and explore international vulnerabilities.

Magnanimity as a Speculation:

Generosity has arisen as a remarkable element of extremely rich person speculation portfolios. Some high-total assets people decisively distribute assets to altruistic undertakings that line up with their qualities and long haul cultural objectives. This not just fills in as a type of expanded interest in friendly effect yet additionally improves the giver's heritage and notoriety.

Risk The executives and Versatile Systems:

Very rich person financial backers figure out the certainty of dangers in worldwide endeavors. Executing risk the executives systems and remaining versatile to showcase elements are significant parts of their speculation approach. This might include supporting methodologies, broadening inside resource classes, and effectively observing international and monetary patterns to settle on informed choices.

In the domain of worldwide endeavors, tycoons utilize a complex way to deal with differentiate their speculation portfolios. This goes past customary resource classes, including worldwide speculations, funding, confidential value, and magnanimity. The capacity to explore the intricacies of the worldwide market and oversee chances recognizes these financial backers, displaying their discernment in profiting by assorted open doors. As the monetary scene keeps on developing, the procedures utilized by very rich person large young men act as an outline for financial backers seeking to accomplish supported development and flexibility in their portfolios.

Chapter 8

Navigating High-Stakes

Strategies Employed by Billionaire Big Boys""

In the dynamic and unstable scene of high-stakes monetary business sectors, the procedures utilized via prepared financial backers, frequently alluded to as "Very rich person Enormous Young men," assume a urgent part in molding market drifts and impacting worldwide economies. This talk dives into the complex techniques these clever people utilize to explore high-stakes showcases effectively. Their philosophies are described by a mix of monetary sharpness, risk the board, and key premonition, making them powerful players in the worldwide financial field.

Monetary Astuteness and Inside and out Investigation:

Tycoon financial backers are famous for their intense monetary sharpness, sharpened through long stretches of involvement and a complete comprehension of market elements. Thorough examination of market patterns, financial pointers, and company basics is a foundation of their dynamic cycle. These shrewd financial backers influence refined monetary instruments, state of the art innovation, and a group of specialists to lead top to bottom examination, empowering them to recognize worthwhile open doors and relieve takes a chance in high-stakes markets.

Risk The executives Systems:

Exploring high-stakes showcases innately implies an elevated degree of hazard. Very rich person financial backers are adroit at executing extensive gamble the board procedures to defend their abundance and amplify returns. Enhancement, a vital precept of their methodology, includes spreading speculations across different resource classes and geographic districts to relieve fixation risk. Furthermore, these financial backers utilize progressed risk displaying methods, intently screen market liquidity, and execute opportune supporting systems to protect their portfolios from unanticipated market changes.

Vital Long haul Vision:

Tycoon Large Young men are famous for their vital long haul vision, which directs their venture choices in the midst of market unpredictability. They have the premonition to recognize arising patterns, troublesome advances, and groundbreaking business sector shifts. This essential vision empowers them to situate themselves on the ball, exploiting open doors that may not be promptly evident to the more extensive market. By adjusting their ventures to long haul worldwide monetary patterns, these financial backers exhibit a promise to practical abundance creation.

Flexibility and Crafty Financial planning:

Effective route of high-stakes markets requires flexibility and a readiness to benefit from unexpected open doors. Tycoon financial backers display a deft methodology, quickly changing their portfolios in light of changing economic situations. Their sharp outlook permits them to use market separations, monetary slumps, or industry disturbances to obtain resources at good valuations. By staying light-footed, these financial backers exploit market failures, transforming difficulties into rewarding open doors.

All in all, the systems utilized by Very rich person Huge Young men in exploring high-stakes markets are a demonstration of their monetary ability, risk the board sharpness, vital vision, and flexibility. Through fastidious investigation, an emphasis on long haul objectives, and a deft outlook, these financial backers face the hardships of market instability as well as arise as compelling planners of worldwide monetary patterns. Concentrating on their procedures gives significant experiences to hopeful financial backers and monetary experts planning to explore and prevail in the mind boggling territory of high-stakes monetary business sectors.

Chapter 9

The Art of Networking

Building Relationships and Alliances in Billionaire Circles""

In the powerful scene of contemporary business, the capacity to develop significant connections and partnerships is a crucial expertise that recognizes effective business people from their companions. No place is this more obvious than in the rarified demeanor of extremely rich person circles, where the specialty of systems administration takes on an uplifted importance. The capacity to interface, team up, and produce partnerships with persuasive people isn't just a demonstration of one's social keenness but on the other hand is an essential basic for those meaning to explore the mind boggling universe of high-stakes business.

Grasping the Elements of Very rich person Circles:

Extremely rich person circles are selective environments where the combination of riches, influence, and impact makes an interesting social dynamic. Organizing inside these circles includes exploring a scene where prudence, trust, and shared values assume essential parts. Laying out and supporting connections in such a climate requires a nuanced comprehension of the people in question, their needs, and the unwritten standards that oversee these tip top circles.

Key Standards of Systems administration in Very rich person Circles:

Realness and Trustworthiness: In very rich person circles, validness is a money that holds enormous worth. Building connections in light of truthfulness and uprightness encourages trust, a foundation of fruitful systems administration. Keeping a reliable and straightforward disposition upgrades one's standing as well as guarantees long haul believability inside these elite circles.

Key Relationship Building: Systems administration in tycoon circles isn't about amount however quality. Key relationship building includes recognizing key people whose values line up with one's own and whose impact can catalyze commonly gainful open doors. This essential methodology guarantees that associations are significant and add to individual and expert development.

Developing a Different Organization: Variety in an organization is a wellspring of solidarity. Tycoon circles incorporate a wide range of enterprises, and a balanced organization mirrors a different scope of points of view and skill. Effectively searching out associations from various areas expands one's information base and opens ways to imaginative coordinated efforts.

Powerful Relational abilities: Clear and successful correspondence is fundamental in tycoon circles, where accuracy and brevity are exceptionally esteemed. Articulating thoughts, communicating desires, and effectively paying attention to others are basic parts of fruitful systems administration. Becoming the best at correspondence improves one's capacity to convey worth and cultivate significant associations.

Correspondence and Liberality: The ethos of correspondence is profoundly imbued in tycoon circles. Developing a mentality of liberality, whether through sharing bits of knowledge, assets, or associations, makes a culture of common help. Demonstrations of liberality reinforce existing connections as well as establish the groundwork for future collusions.

In the domain of extremely rich person circles, the specialty of systems administration rises above simple social connection; it turns into an essential basic for those expecting to flourish in a climate where impact and prosperity meet. By embracing genuineness, key reasoning, variety, powerful correspondence, and a feeling of correspondence, people can explore these elite circles with artfulness. Building connections and collusions in very rich person circles isn't only an end in itself; it is a way to open phenomenal open doors and add to the aggregate progress of a chosen handful at the zenith of the business world.

Chapter 10

From Startups to Unicorns

Analyzing the Billionaire Big Boys' Success Stories in Tech and Innovation"

In the powerful scene of the innovation and development area, the excursion from humble starting points as new businesses to accomplishing the sought after "unicorn" status addresses a story of versatility, advancement, and key ability. This investigation dives into the examples of overcoming adversity of tech monsters that have changed from new companies to unicorns, unwinding the key factors that pushed them to the echelons of extremely rich person status. Understanding these examples of overcoming adversity gives priceless experiences yearning for business visionaries, financial backers, and industry lovers looking to explore the mind boggling landscape of the tech world.

Exploring the Startup Environment:

The excursion starts with a profound plunge into the startup biological system, where visionary business people leave on a journey to address neglected needs and disturb customary ventures. These trailblazers exhibit an intense comprehension of market holes, utilizing their inventiveness and specialized discernment to devise arrangements that reverberate with customers. Contextual investigations of notable new companies like Airbnb, Uber, and Dropbox act as convincing representations of pioneers distinguishing undiscovered open doors and creating imaginative plans of action.

Developing Development as an Upper hand:

At the core of the change from new businesses to unicorns lies a steady obligation to advancement. Fruitful tech organizations consistently push the limits of what is conceivable, presenting earth shattering advances and administrations that rethink enterprises. Looking at the development techniques of organizations like Tesla, SpaceX, and Palantir divulges the significance of cultivating a culture that energizes trial and error, embraces disappointment as a venturing stone to progress, and stays in front of developing business sector patterns.

Key Subsidizing and Venture Scene:

A basic empowering influence of the excursion to unicorn status is exploring the mind boggling universe of subsidizing and ventures. Fruitful organizations proficiently secure financing at urgent stages, falling in line with vital financial backers who give capital as well as offer priceless ability and organizations of real value. Investigating financing rounds and venture methodologies of organizations like Stripe, Robinhood, and Coinbase reveals insight into the harmonious connection among new businesses and financial backers, highlighting the meaning of all around coordinated capital implantations.

Worldwide Development and Market Entrance:

The development from new companies to unicorns is many times joined by an essential spotlight on worldwide extension. Organizations that effectively scale universally show an intense comprehension of different business sectors, adjusting their items and administrations to meet the remarkable requirements of a worldwide client base. Concentrating on the extension techniques of organizations like Alibaba, Tencent, and ByteDance highlights the significance of a worldwide outlook, social responsiveness, and deft versatility to differing administrative scenes.

Exploring Difficulties and Adjusting to Change:

The way to unicorn status is laden with difficulties, from administrative obstacles to serious contest. Effective tech organizations display an exceptional capacity to explore these difficulties, utilizing versatility and strength as key resources. Investigating how organizations like Netflix, Amazon, and Facebook turned because of misfortune gives significant examples on remaining light-footed, responsive, and focused on long haul objectives.

The excursion from new companies to unicorns in the domain of tech and development is a diverse story that entwines vision, advancement, key organizations, and a tenacious quest for greatness. Dissecting the examples of overcoming adversity of extremely rich person huge young men in the business offers a guide for arising business people, featuring the significance of imagination, flexibility, and an undaunted obligation to taking care of true issues. As the innovation scene keeps on developing, these examples of overcoming adversity act as signals of motivation for those graphing their course through the dynamic and cutthroat universe of tech business venture.

Chapter 11

The Disruptive Innovations of Billionaire Big Boys:

Unraveling Tech's Game-Changing Entrepreneurs"

In the unique domain of innovation, a select gathering of visionary business people has arisen as the main impetus behind problematic developments that reshape ventures and rethink the actual texture of our computerized scene. Named the "Very rich person Enormous Young men," these tech titans have amassed immense fortunes as well as altered the manner in which we live, work, and communicate. This article digs into the groundbreaking effect of these people, investigating the problematic advancements that have shot them to the highest point of the business world.

Elon Musk: Spearheading the Fate of Transportation and Energy

Quite possibly of the most noticeable figure in the tech field, Elon Musk, has left permanent imprints across various businesses. Tesla, Musk's brainchild, has changed the auto area with electric vehicles that mix maintainability and execution. Furthermore, Musk's endeavors into space investigation with SpaceX have re-imagined the conceivable outcomes of interplanetary travel, while his undertakings with SolarCity and the Exhausting Organization signal a change in outlook in clean energy and metropolitan foundation.

Jeff Bezos: Reshaping Business and Then some

The pioneer behind Amazon, Jeff Bezos, has reclassified the retail scene, changing it into a computerized commercial center monster. His visionary way to deal with internet business has upset customary retail as well as stretched out into distributed computing with Amazon Web Administrations (AWS). Bezos' quest for development stretches out to the avionic business through Blue Beginning, displaying his obligation to pushing the limits of human space investigation.

Mark Zuckerberg: Associating the World through Web-based Entertainment

Mark Zuckerberg, the prime supporter of Facebook, plays had an essential impact in forming the manner in which we interface and offer data. Facebook's worldwide effect on interpersonal interaction is unrivaled, impacting correspondence, governmental issues, and business. With acquisitions like Instagram and WhatsApp, Zuckerberg's problematic vision stretches out past the bounds of a solitary stage, making an interconnected computerized biological system that arrives at billions.

Satya Nadella: Changing Microsoft's Inheritance

As the President of Microsoft, Satya Nadella has directed the organization into another period of development. Embracing distributed computing and man-made consciousness, Nadella has renewed Microsoft's significance in the tech business. The procurement of LinkedIn and GitHub, alongside an emphasis on open-source drives, mirrors Nadella's obligation to encouraging joint effort and driving innovative progressions.

Jack Mama: Changing Internet business and Money

Jack Mama, the organizer behind Alibaba Gathering, has been a pioneer in the internet business space, changing how business is led universally. Alibaba's foundation have enabled private companies as well as differentiated into areas, for example, distributed computing and advanced finance through Insect Gathering. Mama's impact stretches out to magnanimity and training, representing a comprehensive way to deal with cultural effect.

The troublesome advancements led by the Tycoon Enormous Young men have made a permanent imprint on the tech business and then some. From electric vehicles and space investigation to long range interpersonal communication and web based business, these visionaries have reclassified the limits of what is conceivable. As their organizations proceed to develop and redefine known limits, the effect of these tech titans on our interconnected world is probably going to shape the future in manners we can start to envision. The continuous adventure of their troublesome developments fills in as a demonstration of the groundbreaking force of enterprising vision in the consistently developing scene of innovation.

Chapter 12

Strategies of Success

Decoding the Business Acumen of Billionaire Tech Tycoons"

The climb of very rich person tech investors has become inseparable from advancement, interruption, and unrivaled achievement. These visionary chiefs have not just upset the manner in which we live and work however have likewise started a trend for accomplishing remarkable accomplishments in the business world. This investigation means to take apart the procedures that have pushed these people to the apex of progress, giving bits of knowledge into the business sharpness that has characterized their professions.

Visionary Initiative:

One consistent idea among very rich person tech magnates is their capacity to imagine the future and expect market patterns. Visionary initiative includes the ability to recognize open doors before they become standard and to diagram a course that others may not as yet see. Pioneers like Elon Musk, Jeff Bezos, and Stamp Zuckerberg have exhibited an uncanny capacity to appropriately predict the direction of innovation and position their organizations.

Development as a Center Precept:

Advancement is the soul of the tech business, and effective moguls perceive its fundamental significance. These pioneers cultivate conditions that energize imagination, risk-taking, and the quest for weighty thoughts. Macintosh's late prime supporter, Steve Occupations, was famous for his fixation on development, stressing the making of items that meet as well as surpass client assumptions. This obligation to development has pushed organizations higher than ever as well as re-imagined ventures.

Versatile Strength:

The tech scene is famous for its dynamism and fast changes. Very rich person tech head honchos display a special capacity to explore through vulnerabilities, adjusting their procedures to address developing difficulties. Satya Nadella's extraordinary authority at Microsoft, for example, embodies the force of versatile strength. Under his direction, the organization moved its concentration from a customary programming way to deal with a cloud-driven model, exhibiting the significance of being nimble in a quickly changing business climate.

Client Driven Approach:

A critical part of the outcome of tech moguls lies in their relentless obligation to understanding and tending to client needs. By focusing on client experience and consistently refining items and administrations in view of criticism, these pioneers major areas of strength for produce with their client base. Amazon's Jeff Bezos, for example, has been a backer of putting the client first, driving the organization's client driven culture and its tenacious quest for greatness in help conveyance.

Key Organizations and Consolidations:

Vital joint efforts and consolidations have been instrumental in the examples of overcoming adversity of numerous tech magnates. By fashioning associations that supplement their assets and gaining organizations with important resources, these pioneers extend their impact and expand their contributions. Letter set Inc's. Google, under the initiative of Sundar Pichai, has decisively gained various organizations, improving its portfolio and cementing its situation as a tech goliath.

The procedures utilized by very rich person tech moguls address a rich embroidery of visionary initiative, development, versatile strength, client centricity, and key organizations. Hopeful business people and business pioneers can draw motivation from these illuminators, perceiving that outcome in the powerful tech industry requires an all encompassing and ground breaking approach. By disentangling the business discernment of these tech titans, one can gather significant examples that rise above ventures, encouraging an outlook helpful for groundbreaking outcome in the present consistently developing business scene.

Chapter 13

From Garage to Glory

Tracing the Start-up Origins of Billionaire Tech Titans"

Digging into the convincing story of 'From Carport to Brilliance: Following the Beginning up Starting points of Extremely rich person Tech Titans,' this extensive investigation fastidiously follows the modest starting points of visionary business people who changed creative thoughts hatched in carport spaces into billion-dollar tech domains, offering a nuanced comprehension of the vital minutes and key choices that impelled them from haziness to extraordinary outcome in the powerful scene of the innovation business."

The excursion from humble starting points in a carport to the zenith of progress has turned into an unbelievable story in the tech business. A considerable lot of the present very rich person tech titans began their pioneering adventures in the most honest spaces, demonstrating that development and assurance can change little thoughts into worldwide realms. This investigation into the startup beginnings of these tech magnates discloses not just the coarseness and energy that energized their prosperity yet additionally the essential choices that transformed carport new companies into billion-dollar endeavors.

Visionary Advancement:

The beneficial excursion frequently starts with a visionary thought that rocks the boat. Investigating how tech titans conceptualized momentous advancements in their carports reveals insight into the innovative approach that birthed problematic advancements. By understanding the beginning of these thoughts, hopeful business people can draw motivation for their own endeavors, figuring out how to distinguish open doors where others see difficulties.

Lean Beginning up Approach:

From restricted assets to strict financial plans, carport new businesses frequently work under limitations that compel them to take on the lean beginning up system. This part investigates how tech titans streamlined their activities, focused on fundamental undertakings, and iterated rapidly to accomplish item market fit. These illustrations in proficiency and versatility are important for business visionaries hoping to develop adaptable organizations starting from the earliest stage.

Vital Associations:

Joint effort has been a vital driver in the progress of numerous tech titans. Dissecting how these business visionaries produced vital organizations, both inside and outside their enterprises, gives bits of knowledge into the force of systems administration and cooperation. Understanding how to recognize and use reciprocal qualities can be a distinct advantage for new businesses planning to quickly scale.

Client Driven Plan:

Client experience and configuration thinking play played vital parts in the victory of tech titans. This part investigates how these business visionaries focused on client driven plan all along, making items and administrations that reverberate with their interest group. By inspecting their client centered procedures, hopeful new businesses can figure out how to fabricate client faithfulness and lay out serious areas of strength for a presence.

Development Sparkles in Humble Settings:

The origination of numerous tech domains can be followed back to the honest environmental factors of a carport. The narrative of Steve Occupations and Steve Wozniak establishing Mac in a rural carport is a perfect representation. Featuring the meaning of these modest starting points adds a profound touch as well as highlights the grassroots idea of these tech goliaths.

From Apartment to Meeting room: The School Start-Up Peculiarity:

Numerous tech magnates launched their enterprising excursions while still in school. The apartments of Silicon Valley are amazing in encouraging advancement. Mark Zuckerberg's production of Facebook from his Harvard apartment is a famous representation. Investigating how these youthful personalities explored moves and utilized their scholarly surroundings to fabricate historic innovations gives significant bits of knowledge.

Changing Ventures: The Troublesome Force of Tech New companies:

These carport conceived organizations didn't simply make items; they disturbed whole ventures. Amazon's Jeff Bezos started his internet business realm by selling books on the web. Tesla's

Chapter 14

Venture Capital Alchemy

Unveiling the Investment Magic Behind Billionaire Tech Fortunes"

Funding Speculative chemistry remains at the crossing point of advancement and venture, unwinding the secretive and frequently rewarding world that has moved various business visionaries into the echelons of extremely rich person status. This article digs into the complexities of funding, analyzing the venture procedures and dynamic cycles that have changed pivotal thoughts into billion-dollar tech fortunes.

The Beginning of Funding: The underlying foundations of investment can be followed back to the mid-twentieth 100 years, when trailblazers like Georges Doriot and Arthur Rock established the groundwork for a venture model that tried to subsidize and support beginning phase, high-expected organizations. Throughout the long term, investment has developed into a powerful power, molding the scene of the innovation business by filling the development of organizations that have reclassified how we live, work, and convey.

The Catalytic Cycle: Financial speculators are similar to advanced chemists, having the capacity to transform promising thoughts into amazing chances. The interaction starts with fastidious reasonable level of effort, where financial backers investigate each part of a startup - from the practicality of its plan of action to the skill of its initiative group. This catalytic examination reaches out to the market potential, serious scene, and versatility of the endeavor.

Key Speculations: Effective financial speculators are capable at recognizing and decisively putting resources into organizations that have problematic advancements or imaginative answers for existing issues. They explore the unpredictable scene of the startup biological system, perceiving the extraordinary capability of a beginning thought and its capacity to reshape whole enterprises. These essential ventures frequently require a sharp comprehension of market patterns, innovative progressions, and a prescience that rises above the ongoing industry scene.

The Force of Mentorship and Systems administration: Funding goes past the simple implantation of assets; it includes a cooperative connection among financial backers and business visionaries. Prepared investors frequently offer something other than monetary sponsorship that would be useful - they offer mentorship, direction, and a huge organization of industry associations. This mentorship is a vital piece of the catalytic interaction, catalyzing the development and advancement of new businesses as they explore the difficulties of scaling their activities.

Alleviating Dangers: Funding isn't without gambles, and effective financial backers figure out the sensitive harmony among hazard and award. Catalytic dominance in this domain includes the essential broadening of venture portfolios, keen gamble the executives, and a profound comprehension of the developing business sector elements. The capacity to relieve gambles while jumping all over chances is a sign of the best financial speculators.

Funding Speculative chemistry addresses an exceptional mix of instinct, skill, and key foreknowledge, changing creative thoughts into the billion-dollar tech fortunes that characterize our period. As the innovation scene keeps on developing, financial speculators stay at the very front of driving change, supporting visionary business people, and uncovering the catalytic insider facts that transform new companies into worldwide goliaths. Understanding the subtleties of this speculation enchantment gives significant experiences into the unique universe of investment and the speculative chemistry that fills the production of tech tycoons.

Chapter 15

Global Titans

The International Expansion Strategies of Billionaire Tech Moguls"

In the steadily developing scene of the worldwide innovation industry, the rising of tycoon tech head honchos has been downright fantastic. As these titans of advancement accumulate riches and impact, their desires reach out a long ways past public lines. This point by point investigation dives into the worldwide development methodologies utilized by these tech magnates, revealing insight into the mind boggling trap of choices, organizations, and ventures that shape their worldwide impression.

Key Vision and Worldwide Yearnings:

The excursion of these tech head honchos frequently starts with a visionary viewpoint that rises above homegrown business sectors. A guarantee to tackling worldwide difficulties and a faith in the comprehensiveness of their items or administrations drive their worldwide ambitions.Case Study: Elon Musk's SpaceX, with its interplanetary desires, embodies the worldwide vision that rises above earthbound limits.

Market Passage Approaches:

Tech investors take on assorted market passage methodologies, going from acquisitions and associations to laying out auxiliaries or completely claimed substances. The choice of the passage mode is complicatedly attached to the administrative climate, social subtleties, and market elements of the objective country.Case Study: Amazon's procurement of Entire Food varieties denoted an essential introduction to the retail area, joining its internet business ability with an actual presence.

Social Variation and Confinement:

Adjusting items and administrations to nearby societies is a significant component in effective global extension. Tech magnates put resources into understanding social subtleties and fitting their contributions to reverberate with different audiences.Case Study: Netflix's restriction of content across dialects and social settings has been instrumental in its worldwide endorser development.

Exploring Administrative Scenes:

The administrative climate changes altogether across nations, presenting difficulties for worldwide development. Tech big shots utilize legitimate and administrative specialists to explore these intricacies and guarantee consistence with nearby laws.Case Study: Google's persistent commitment with administrative bodies overall delineates the significance of a proactive way to deal with consistence and strategy.

Interest in Developing Business sectors:

Recognizing and putting resources into developing business sectors is a typical system for tech investors hoping to benefit from undiscovered capacity. These business sectors frequently present remarkable difficulties yet in addition offer significant development opportunities.Case Study: Facebook's designated interests in network drives in developing business sectors, like Africa, mirror a drawn out obligation to growing its client base.

Advancement and Exploration Centers:

Laying out advancement and examination center points in essential areas permits tech tycoons to take advantage of worldwide ability pools and remain in front of industry patterns. These centers act as hatcheries for state of the art advancements and cultivate cooperation with neighborhood talent.Case Study: Microsoft's worldwide organization of examination focuses empowers the organization to outfit the mastery of different scientists and architects, adding to its development environment.

End:

The global extension systems of very rich person tech head honchos are complex, requiring a sensitive equilibrium of vision, flexibility, and vital keenness. As these worldwide titans keep on molding the eventual fate of innovation on an overall scale, their methodologies give important experiences to hopeful business people and industry eyewitnesses the same. The transaction of development, social responsiveness, administrative keenness, and vital speculations structure the foundation of their progress in the worldwide field, denoting a change in outlook in the customary limits of business extension.